THIS IS AN ANT!

DID YOU KNOW...
Ants are super strong! If you had the strength of an ant, you would be able to pick up an elephant!

DID YOU FIND ANY ANTS TODAY?

HOW MANY ANTS DID YOU FIND TODAY?

THIS IS A BEE!

DID YOU KNOW...
Bees make honey! The bees use honey to feed their young, so they have something to eat all winter long!

DID YOU FIND ANY BEES TODAY?

HOW MANY BEES DID YOU FIND TODAY?

THIS IS A SNAIL!

DID YOU KNOW...
Snails can live up to 20 years old, which is probably good since they move so slowly; it may take them that long to get around!

DID YOU FIND ANY SNAILS TODAY?

HOW MANY SNAILS DID YOU FIND TODAY?

DID YOU KNOW...
Farmers love ladybugs because they eat plant-eating pests. A single ladybug can eat thousands of these pests in just one year!

DID YOU FIND ANY LADYBUGS TODAY?

HOW MANY LADYBUGS
DID YOU FIND TODAY?

DID YOU KNOW...
Not all spiders spin webs to catch other insects! Some spiders hunt their prey and pounce like a cat!

DID YOU FIND ANY SPIDERS TODAY?

HOW MANY SPIDERS DID YOU FIND TODAY?

DID YOU KNOW...
Butterflies can't bite or chew! They use their long, tube-like tongues to slurp!
Just like you would with a straw!

DID YOU FIND ANY BUTTERFLIES TODAY?

HOW MANY BUTTERFLIES
DID YOU FIND TODAY?

THIS IS A GRASSHOPPER!

DID YOU KNOW...
Male grasshoppers sing!
They sing by rubbing their wings or hind legs against their front wings!

DID YOU FIND ANY
GRASSHOPPERS TODAY?

HOW MANY GRASSHOPPERS
DID YOU FIND TODAY?

THIS IS A DRAGONFLY!

DID YOU KNOW...
Dragonflies are expert fliers!
Flying in every direction possible, they can hover in midair like a helicopter.

DID YOU FIND ANY DRAGONFLIES TODAY?

HOW MANY DRAGONFLIES DID YOU FIND TODAY?

THIS IS A FLY!

DID YOU KNOW...

Flies can see in all directions! Up, down, left, right, below and above all at once! That is why they are so hard to catch!

DID YOU FIND ANY FLIES TODAY?

HOW MANY FLIES DID YOU FIND TODAY?

THIS IS A CATERPILLAR!

DID YOU KNOW...
Caterpillars consume as much as 30,000 times their body size in food! That's what helps them grow into butterflies!

DID YOU FIND ANY CATERPILLAR TODAY?

HOW MANY CATERPILLARS DID YOU FIND TODAY?

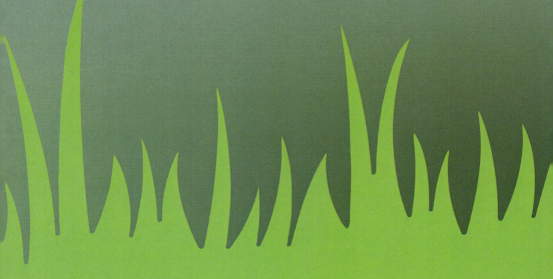

Made in United States
North Haven, CT
07 April 2025